Witnesses of
CHRISTMAS

A Musical Journey through the Nativity of

Jesus the Christ

All Part I sheet music, Jenny Oaks Baker & Family Four accompaniment tracks, and Christmas recordings arranged by Kurt Bestor.

Vocals on "Angels We Have Heard on High," "O Come, O Come Emmanuel," and "Do You Hear What I Hear?" by Alex Sharpe.

Part II songs "What Wondrous Love Is This?" "I Need Thee Every Hour," "More Holiness Give Me," and "Finlandia" arranged by Sam Cardon.

Part II songs "Amazing Grace" and "He Lives: Theme from *The Lamb of God*" arranged by Kurt Bestor.

Text © 2023 Jason F. Wright and Jenny Oaks Baker

Artwork:

"Nativity Triptych" © Annie Henrie Nader.

"A Light to the Gentiles" © Greg Olsen.

"Journey to Bethlehem" and "Silent Night" © Joseph F. Brickey.

"Be It unto Me" © Liz Lemon Swindle. Image courtesy of Havenlight.

"For unto Us a Child Is Born" and "His Name Shall Be Called Wonderful" by Simon Dewey. Courtesy of altusfineart.com © 2023.

Visit us at ShadowMountain.com

Ensign Peak is an imprint of Shadow Mountain Publishing, LLC.

Library of Congress Cataloging-in-Publication Data

Names: Wright, Jason F., author. | Baker, Jenny Oaks, author. | Family Four (Musical group: Jenny Oaks Baker)

Title: Witnesses of Christmas: a musical journey through the nativity of Jesus the Christ / Jason F. Wright, Jenny Oaks Baker & Family Four.

Description: Salt Lake City: Shadow Mountain, [2023] | Includes bibliographical references. |

Summary: "New York Times bestselling author Jason F. Wright joins with Jenny Oaks Baker & Family Four to present a musical journey through the Nativity of Jesus the Christ"—Provided by publisher.

Identifiers: LCCN 2023009713 | ISBN 9781639931712 (hardback)

Subjects: LCSH: Jesus Christ—Nativity—Drama. | Christian life. | BISAC: RELIGION / Holidays / Christmas & Advent | LCGFT: Christmas plays. | Carols. | Gift books.

Classification: LCC PN6120. C5 W75 2023 | DDC 812/.6—dc23/eng/20230413

LC record available at https: //lccn.loc.gov/2023009713

Printed in China

RR Donnelley, Dongguan, China 4/2023

10 9 8 7 6 5 4 3 2 1

Witnesses of CHRISTMAS

A Musical Journey through the Nativity of
Jesus the Christ

JASON F. WRIGHT

JENNY OAKS BAKER
& FAMILY FOUR

ENSIGN PEAK

We dedicate this project to the One who makes all things possible—our Savior and yours—Jesus Christ.

Contents

INTRODUCTION

Dear Friends,

What does it mean to truly testify of Jesus Christ and to become witnesses of Him and the day we honor His miraculous birth?

In today's increasingly troubled and turbulent times, what can we personally do to faithfully follow and to become more dedicated disciples of our Savior?

The answer for Jenny Oaks Baker came in a gradual flood of inspiration in the fall of 2020. There was no more time to wait. With spiritual urgency, Jenny invited her family and willing friends to spend the holidays boldly witnessing of Him through scriptures, storytelling, song, and dance.

A phone call with Jason Wright would change their lives forever. As Jenny became performer, producer, and everything in between, Jason wrote a script and created a character that would invite audiences to experience the beauty of Jesus's birth in Bethlehem. Combining Jenny and her accomplished children with dancers and choirs, percussion and lighting, visuals and videos, a show was born.

It became *Joy to the World: A Sacred Celebration*.

Since premiering that year with a single performance, with Jason narrating as a shepherd named David, and with Jenny at center stage surrounded by her family, the show has grown into a traveling production that's welcomed thousands of performers of all ages to the stage. The unique experience has been enjoyed by hundreds of thousands around the country, and we're humbled by the response of so many Christians who have made the evening a part of their family Christmas traditions.

Perhaps this book will play a similar role.

Whether just once or for years to come, we hope our multimedia message strengthens your faith in Jesus and adds color to your celebrations. We express our gratitude to the team at Shadow Mountain Publishing for seeing the vision and believing in the power of that wonderful word—*witness*.

We invite you to gather with family, friends, book clubs, and church groups to experience the music and written word. We hope you'll even select your own narrator shepherd, and may you sing, share, and testify!

Finally, it is often said that Jesus is the reason for the season. May we lovingly adjust that axiom? The truth, of course, is that He is the reason for every season, every day, every moment. He is the reason for everything at every time in every place.

Together we witness that Jesus Christ is the One, the Way, the Hope, the Light, the Love. May we ever testify of Him, His mission, His miracles.

Indeed, may we all become witnesses of Christmas.

With love,

Jason, Jenny & Family Four

Part I

Joy to the World
A SACRED CELEBRATION

Our Invitation

As we begin, please invite and welcome your family and friends together. Bake some cookies, warm up your voices and some hot cocoa, and if you've got a pianist in the group, get those fingers ready to dance.

A musical journey awaits!

Let the show begin!

Please enjoy this adaptation of the narration and music from the original stage production of *Joy to the World: A Sacred Celebration*.

With a narrator playing the role of David, along with traditional group caroling, and by using the provided QR codes with musical tracks and videos, we pray you'll enjoy this taste of what a shepherd saw in Bethlehem.

Friends—welcome to Bethlehem!

I'm grateful you're here to witness the night the Savior of the world was born.

The night the world changed forever.

My name is David, and I'm a shepherd.

No, not the famous David.

I'm not nearly that brave.

But I do have a story to tell.

Remember when Luke wrote that "there were in the same country shepherds abiding in the field, keeping watch over their flock by night"?

That's me.

I was among those shepherds.

Yes, I was a witness.

And tonight, I want to share a glimpse of what we saw.

I want you to become witnesses with me.

Through both sacred scriptures and majestic music that come from heaven, we can become a bolder body of believers.

As we begin, I pray you'll allow yourselves to experience more with this book than you may have imagined.

I pray you'll have eyes to see and ears to hear a heavenly message meant just for you.

YES, TOGETHER WE WILL SING and listen to some marvelous music, but the real show, the one you'll remember long after the final page, won't take place on paper—it will happen within you.

So, if you're willing to be a witness with me, willing to embrace all Jesus Christ has for you to feel and to learn, then we start at the very beginning, with the Angels We Have Heard on High and our heartfelt plea to Come, O Come Emmanuel.

Angels We Have Heard on High

Music and Videos

O Come, O Come, Emmanuel

Music and Videos

Angels We Have Heard on High

Joyfully ♩ = 104

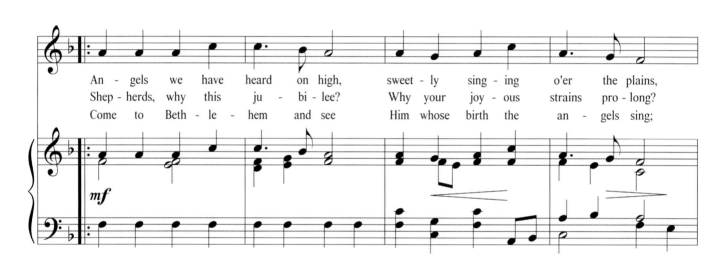

An - gels we have heard on high, sweet - ly sing - ing o'er the plains,
Shep - herds, why this ju - bi - lee? Why your joy - ous strains pro - long?
Come to Beth - le - hem and see Him whose birth the an - gels sing;

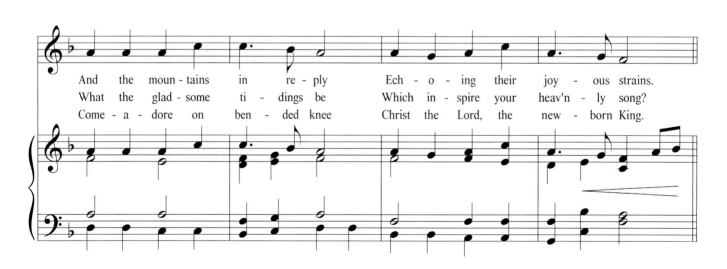

And the moun - tains in re - ply Ech - o - ing their joy - ous strains.
What the glad - some ti - dings be Which in - spire your heav'n - ly song?
Come a - dore on ben - ded knee Christ the Lord, the new - born King.

Text: French carol, ca. 1862
Music: French carol
Arranged by: Kurt Bestor

O Come, O Come, Emmanuel

Text: Unknown 12th century author
Music: Adapted from 15th century French processional
Arranged by: Kurt Bestor

Luke 2

And it came to pass in those days, that there went out a decree from Caesar Augustus, that all the world should be taxed. . . .

And all went to be taxed, every one into his own city.

And Joseph also went up from Galilee, out of the city of Nazareth, into Judaea, unto the city of David, which is called Bethlehem; . . . to be taxed with Mary his espoused wife, being great with child.

It's true, this beautiful story of Luke 2.

Every shepherd that night witnessed that the child Mary carried was no ordinary son, but the Only Begotten Son of God, even Jesus the Christ.

My friends, you can witness too.

Of Him, of His perfect plan.

Simply Come, All Ye Faithful.

OH, COME, ALL YE FAITHFUL

Music and Videos

OH, COME, ALL YE FAITHFUL

Moderato ♩ = 94

Oh, come, all ye faith - ful, joy - ful and tri - um - phant! Oh,
Sing, choirs of an - gels, Sing in ex - ul - ta - tion; ____
Yea, Lord, we greet thee, Born this hap - py morn - ing; ____

come ye, oh come ____ ye to Beth - le - hem.
Sing, all ye cit - i - zens of Hea - ven a - bove!
Je - sus to thee ____ be all glo - ry giv'n.

Text & Music: Attr. to John F. Wade, ca. 1711–1786
Arranged by: Kurt Bestor

Luke 2

And so it was, that, while they were there, the days were accomplished that she should be delivered.

And she brought forth her firstborn son, and wrapped him in swaddling clothes, and laid him in a manger; because there was no room for them in the inn.

No room for Him in the inn, but so much room for Him in the world.

In His world.

Along with those other shepherds, I testify that I witnessed a glorious night, a holy night, a Silent Night.

SILENT NIGHT

Music and Videos

SILENT NIGHT

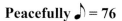

Peacefully ♪ = 76

Si - lent night,   Ho - ly night,   All   is   calm.
Si - lent night,   Ho - ly night   Shep - herds quake
Si - lent night!   Ho - ly night!   Son   of   God,

All   is bright.   Round   yon vir - gin mo - ther and Child,
at   the sight.   Glo - ries stream ___ from hea - ven a - far
love's   pure light   Ra - diant beams ___ from thy ho - ly face,

Ho - ly In - fant so ten - der and mild, Sleep in hea - ven - ly
Heav'n - ly hosts_____ sing "Al - le - lu - ia." Christ the Sa - vior is
with the dawn of re - deem - ing grace, Je - sus, Lord, at the

1. 2.

peace._____ Sleep___ in heav - en - ly peace.
born, _____ Christ___ the Sa - vior is born.
birth. _____

3.

Je - sus, Lord at thy birth; Je - sus, Lord, at thy birth.

Text: Joseph Mohr, 1792–1848
Music: Franz Gruber, 1787–1863
Arranged by: Kurt Bestor

Isn't it glorious?

What a sacred scene we saw. We humble witnesses were in awe at seeing heaven arrive on earth.

Yes, we'd heard the prophecies, we'd hoped the day would come, but being present with the promised Messiah was a gift like no other.

It was an eternal privilege to meet Joseph, Mary, and the Christ child— to breathe this holy air.

Each witness, no matter the size of our flock or our place in the kingdom, told the story of this night, the story of baby Jesus, the story of His birth and His life, for the rest of ours.

Luke 2

And suddenly there was with the angel a multitude of the heavenly host praising God, and saying, Glory to God in the highest, and on earth peace, good will toward men.

And it came to pass, as the angels were gone away from them into heaven, the shepherds said one to another, Let us now go even unto Bethlehem, and see this thing which is come to pass, which the Lord hath made known unto us.

And they came with haste, and found Mary, and Joseph, and the babe lying in a manger.

CONSIDER THE MOMENT!

A perfect Son of a perfect Father coming into the world in the most humble of places to the most humble of parents.

And the witnesses who found the One?

The One who would save us all?

We discovered Him not on a throne, nor swaddled in the world's finest linens, but instead we witnessed Him in perfect humility.

It's no wonder heaven sang!

May we now Hark! The Herald Angels Sing, and then marvel at the miracle that sleeps Away in a Manger.

HARK! THE HERALD ANGELS SING

Music and Videos

AWAY IN A MANGER

Music and Videos

HARK! THE HERALD ANGELS SING

Gloriously ♩ = 102

Hark! the her - ald an - gels sing, __ Glo - ry to the new - born King!
Hail the heav'n - born Prince of Peace! __ Hail the Son of Righ - teous - ness!

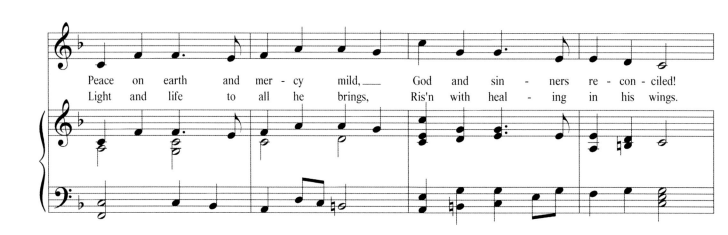

Peace on earth and mer - cy mild, __ God and sin - ners re - con - ciled!
Light and life to all he brings, Ris'n with heal - ing in his wings.

Text: Charles Wesley, 1707–1788
Music: Felix Mendelssohn, 1809–1847
Arranged by: Kurt Bestor

AWAY IN A MANGER

With a Gentle Rocking Motion ♩ = 74

A - way in a __ man - ger, no __ crib for a
cat - tle are __ low - ing; the __ poor ba - by -
near me, Lord __ Je - sus I __ ask Thee to

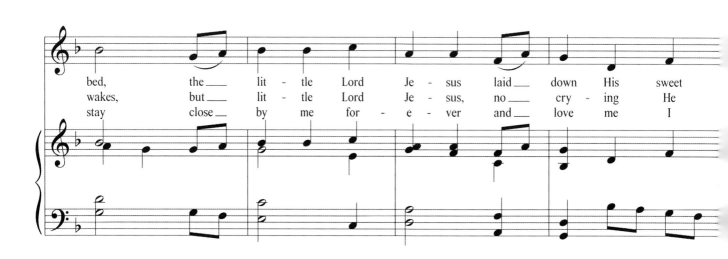

bed, the __ lit - tle Lord Je - sus laid __ down His sweet
wakes, but __ lit - tle Lord Je - sus, no __ cry - ing He
stay close __ by me for - e - ver and __ love me I

Text & Music: Wm. J. Kirkpatrick
Arranged by: Kurt Bestor

WITH SIGNS FILLING THE SKIES, my shepherd friends and I came. Among the most noble and revered were the Magi, with their gifts of gold, frankincense, and myrrh. Though we do not know the precise day they arrived at His feet, we do know they inspired one of America's first and most original Christmas carols. It is the beloved We Three Kings.

WE THREE KINGS

Music and Videos

We Three Kings

Moderato ♪ = 136

We three kings of Or - i - ent are bear - ing gifts we tra - verse a - far.
Born a King on Beth - le - hem plain. Gold I bring to crown Him a - gain.
Frank - in - cense to of - fer have I; In - cense owns a De - i - ty nigh.

Field and foun - tain, moor and moun - tain, fol - low - ing yon - der star. O___
King for e - ver ceas - ing ne - ver o - ver us all to reign.___
Pray'r and prai - sing, all men rai - sing, wor - ship God on high.___

Text & Music: John Henry Hopkins Jr. (1887)
Arranged by: Kurt Bestor

WE WITNESSES FELT SO BLESSED, so chosen.

We were filled with such holy happiness, such gratitude, and such joy.

And here you are, 2,000 years later, still singing this joyful song.

You don't just know the words—they're etched on your hearts.

Joy to the world, the Lord is come;

Let earth receive her King!

Every single time you sing that beautiful refrain, you sing not just joy for yourselves.

No—you sing Joy to the World.

Joy to the World

Music and Videos

JOY TO THE WORLD

Jubilantly ♩ = 86

Joy   to   the world,   the   Lord   is   come;   let   earth   re - ceive   her
Re - joice! Re - joice   when   Je - sus   reigns,   And   Saints   their   songs   em
No   more   will sin   and   sor - row   grow,   Nor   thorns   in - fest   the
Re - joice! Re - joice   in   the   Most   High,   While   Is - rael spreads   a -

King!   Let   ev - 'ry___ heart___   pre - pare   Him___ room,___ And
ploy,   While   fields and___ floods,___ rocks   hills,   and___ plains___ Re -
ground;   He'll   come   and___ make___   the   bless - ings   flow___ Far
broad.   Like   stars___ that   glit___   ter   in___ the___ sky,___ And

Text: Isaac Watts, 1674–1748; alt. by William W. Phelps, 1792–1872
Music: George F. Handel, 1685–1759
Arranged by: Kurt Bestor

THIS DIVINE ARRIVAL, this birth of Jesus Christ as the Only Begotten Son of God, fulfilled promises even older than the land that would raise Him.

And when the baby Jesus came, so also came the world.

Each longing to witness the miracle.

We came to see, to worship, to learn.

We came to celebrate The First Noel.

THE FIRST NOEL

Music and Videos

THE FIRST NOEL

Moderato ♩ = 92

The first___ No - el the an - gel did say Was to cer tain poor
look - ed___ up and saw___ a star Shi - ning in_____ the

shep herds in fields as they lay, In___ fields___ where they lay keep-ing their
East___ be - yond___ them far, And to_____ the___ earth it___ gave___ great

Text & Music: Traditional English carol, ca. 17th century
Arranged by: Kurt Bestor

It's miraculous, isn't it? So many miles and years away from that manger, surrounded by friends and family, we can still feel the love of God.

The Spirit reminds us of the reality of His plan.

We know that Jesus Christ was born—for us—as the literal Son of a living, loving Father.

We know that "Jesus increased in wisdom and stature, and in favour with God and man" (Luke 2:52).

He ministered and performed miracles—for us.

He bled, died, and rose again—for us.

Before the final page, I should confess something.

No, my name isn't David.

And I'm not even a real shepherd.

Honestly, I wouldn't know the difference between a sheep and a goat! I'm just a narrator, and the truth is that as much as I wish I'd been there and seen it all, I didn't.

I'm just like you. I'm a sinner in need of being saved.

And grace, the saving power of Jesus Christ, begins with the Nativity story.

Even though you and I weren't there on that silent and holy night, we each have an opportunity to discover Him in our own time and in our own way. To all of us He extends His invitation to come and seek Jesus, so we can be His disciples and His witnesses.

I wonder . . . as we've journeyed together to Bethlehem, is it possible our eyes have been opened to a lesson of a lifetime? Have we discovered that narrators, like me and my family and friends, don't have to pretend?

WITH PRAYER, with study, and by the great gift of the Holy Spirit, we don't have to see with our physical eyes to be witnesses.

With our spiritual eyes, with our whole soul, we can see.

We can know.

After everything we've witnessed throughout our lives and even on these pages and stages, it's as if we had been there, isn't it?

And now we have the power in us to become His witnesses throughout the world.

We conclude with one of the most important questions in history.

It comes in a whisper, with one voice, but if we will all join in, it can fill the earth this holiday season.

Do You Hear What I Hear?

DO YOU HEAR WHAT I HEAR?

Music and Videos

Do You Hear What I Hear?

Text & Music: Noël Regney (1922–2002) & Shayne Baker (1923–2008)
Arranged by: Kurt Bestor

Part II

Becoming His Witnesses

BY ADOPTING HIS ATTRIBUTES

Therefore, What?

As we celebrate this sacred season and the birth of Jesus Christ, as we recommit ourselves to becoming His witnesses, we might wonder—therefore, what?

Or—what comes next?

Spiritual experiences, those delicate dances with heaven, are meant to change us. What lasting good comes from a moment of clarity with the Holy Ghost if it fades with inaction?

Our journey to become more trustworthy and reliable witnesses of Christ is a path of discipleship. And becoming a disciple is about more than simply being a student. Even the greatest gospel scholars, the doctrinal titans who quote chapter, verse, and history, are not true witnesses if they're not changed by the good news.

Witnesses allow themselves to be changed by truth. They apply what they know. And they recognize that to witness to the world, they need not be perfect. But they do need to desire a deeper relationship with the One who is the divine definition of perfection.

Consider the miracle of our friendship with Jesus. He, being perfect in all things, He being the ultimate witness of the Father and of His plan of happiness, invites our deepest association. He knows, because He paid for our sins, that we're far from perfect. And yet Jesus invites us to walk alongside perfection, to taste it figuratively through His sacred promises and literally through His holy sacraments.

What a gift!

The Only Begotten Son of God comes to us, in our state of sin and imperfection, and says, "Will you be my companion? Would you like to become like me?"

What a friend!

On our never-ending mission to become like Jesus Christ, to become better disciples, we present five Christlike attributes for consideration: benevolence, forgiveness, patience, prayerfulness, and faith.

There are many others, naturally, and you may discover another set of divine principles that draw you closer to the author of your faith. We invite you to share those, as appropriate, with your family, friends, and church groups.

As we explore these attributes and examples of them in action, we'll identify powerful scriptures and then a single word in each that might often be overlooked. We hope these spark discussions and invite insights of your own.

We'll also present five true stories of those who've learned, loved, and lived these attributes. They are presented without names, but their experiences are as real as Jesus of Nazareth.

Finally, we'll suggest five of Jenny's recordings that we believe will enrich your study and worship.

No matter where you are on your walk back to our heavenly home, we testify that every single one of us can become His witnesses by adopting His attributes.

BENEVOLENCE

Pure religion and undefiled before
God and the Father is this, To
VISIT
the fatherless and widows in their affliction,
and to keep himself unspotted from the world.
—James 1:27

What Wondrous Love Is This?

The meaning of *benevolence* is as rich and colorful as the word sounds. It conjures kindness to our thoughts and goodness to our souls. But this attribute isn't simply a state of mind. It's not about kind thoughts or seeing the good in people. It's about doing good to people. It's about blessing our spiritual brothers and sisters.

The word *visit* jumps from the page! It's action! It's a beautiful verb! It inspires us to do more than have an idea or offer a prayer on someone's behalf. It invites us to go and do.

Years ago in a tiny country town, two men found themselves sitting in their car on the side of a quiet road. They'd had an appointment to visit someone from their church family, but the person hadn't answered the door. Instead of returning home feeling defeated, they found a place to pray for another who might need a quick, impromptu *visit*.

The Spirit led them to connect with another friend in another small town twenty miles away. As they drove, they felt an urgency to bring the man a message of hope. They also felt inspired to call and let him know they'd be arriving soon and that they were anxious to *visit*.

Instead of excitement on the other end of the call, they heard drunken despair and hopelessness. He was more than down—he was dejected and emotionally spent. Their friend told them that by the time they arrived, he'd be gone.

Not gone on an errand; gone from this life.

The men called 911 and raced to their friend's side. When they arrived, emergency responders were freeing the man, near death, from a tree on his property. They wept with a combination of sadness and joy as the man was carried past them on a stretcher, briefly took their hands, and was loaded into an ambulance.

Because of their benevolence and desire to *visit* someone in need, a life was preserved, and the faith of everyone involved was strengthened. Over the weeks and months that followed, their friend would receive the help he needed and spend hours talking to the men who saved his life.

In a prayerful moment, these men recognized that benevolence requires more than kind vibes and positivity. It calls for listening, for action, and for love in motion. And, in their case, an emotional and physical *visit*.

Invitation

As you strive to become a better witness, look for ways to show compassion and transform *benevolence* into a beautiful verb. Move beyond thoughts to action.

Other scriptures for consideration:

But a certain Samaritan, as he journeyed, came where he was: and when he saw him, he had compassion on him.
—Luke 10:33

And Jesus went about all Galilee, teaching in their synagogues, and preaching the gospel of the kingdom, and healing all manner of sickness and all manner of disease among the people.
—Matthew 4:23

Forgiveness

But I say unto you, Love your enemies,

bless them that curse you,

DO

good to them that hate you,

and pray for them which despitefully use you,

and persecute you.

—Matthew 5:44

Amazing Grace

Forgiveness is surely among Christ's most difficult attributes to adopt. He asks us to pray, we pray. He asks us to serve, we serve. But when He asks us to forgive, even those who despise, persecute, and curse us, we often resist. Yet His forgiveness of us is endless. He not only forgives our yesterdays, He forgives our todays. And yes, the perfect, spotless Son of God has already forgiven your tomorrows. He's paid for sins we haven't even imagined yet.

Study the word *do* in this well-known verse and consider the possible replacements. We could have been counseled to pause, to ponder, to wait, and to wonder what comes next. He could have simply asked us to love them, bless them, and pray for them. But those would have been more passive steps. Instead, with boldness, we're commanded—not just invited—to *do*. This tiny word packs a spiritual punch!

It is when we *do* that miracles happen. At every opportunity, Jesus was doing His Father's will, doing good, doing the work of His mortal ministry.

This spiritual friendship between the need to forgive and to do something about it is demonstrated by the story of a young woman who recently lost her mother. As a teenager, her mother had literally left her homeless. Plagued by addiction and mental illness, the mother had a breakdown that left her daughter watching her vehicle disappear down the road.

The next few years were not kind to this tender teen. As she was tossed from shelter to shelter and from one foster family to another, she began to doubt her own place in the world. Did she matter to anyone? To her biological mother who'd vanished? Was she invisible to God?

A series of tender mercies led her to a relationship with Jesus Christ and an understanding of forgiveness. She would eventually marry and have children of her own. Then, one day, feeling confident she'd forgiven her absent mother from a distance, she felt the need to do more. Strengthened by the Savior's promise, she reconnected with her mother. But she didn't just invite her for lunch and a visit, she welcomed her mother fully into her and her family's lives.

The remainder of her mother's years were spent doing the things she'd neglected all those years ago. Their home became a sanctuary of love and laughter. When the mother died not long ago, she left this earth the recipient of much good, much forgiveness, and a believer in the power of that wonderful word—*do*.

Invitation

Consider those in your life whom you've struggled to forgive and ask what steps remain for forgiveness to be complete and unconditional, as Christ commands. If there are some you've forgiven in your heart but not aloud, look for appropriate ways to do good and bless their lives.

Other scriptures for consideration:

Come now, and let us reason together, saith the Lord: though your sins be as scarlet, they shall be as white as snow; though they be red like crimson, they shall be as wool.
—Isaiah 1:18

Then said Jesus, Father, forgive them; for they know not what they do. And they parted his raiment, and cast lots.
—Luke 23:34

PATIENCE

REST

in the Lord, and wait patiently for him:

fret not thyself because of him who prospereth in his way,

because of the man who bringeth wicked devices to pass.

Cease from anger, and forsake wrath:

fret not thyself in any wise to do evil.

—Psalm 37:7–8

I Need Thee Every Hour

We're a world in motion. We race from place to place. Even when we're seeking to visit others and to do good, we often run faster than we should. And when storms come and the floods rise, as prophesied and witnessed for thousands of years, we frantically reach for the surface.

But what if we embraced the first word in this beautiful verse? What if in our quest for patience we learned the power of the *rest*? More importantly, resting in the Lord?

When life turns dim and even dark, when life's responsibilities threaten to overwhelm us, when trials wring our hope dry, we need Him more than ever. We pray for relief—now. We pray for blessings—now. We pray for miracles—and we need them yesterday. But isn't Christ's pattern one of patience? Surely, he could have embarked on his ministry ten years earlier. Certainly, he could have spent fewer days and nights fasting in the desert.

Somewhere today, perhaps reading these very words, there's a woman who needed the patience of Job, and who learned the only way to cease anger and forsake wrath was to *rest*. Her trials began with a painful cancer diagnosis of her sweetheart, her best friend, her anchor. Within six months, more news sent her reeling. Her son, her hero, had been killed in an accident. Six months later, this woman's father died. And soon, her husband's battle with cancer came to an end.

Within a year, this faithful woman had lost the three most important men in her life. The trials seemed overwhelming, and loneliness threatened to bury her too. But instead of working harder to heal, rather than finding new reasons to be busy and take her mind off her challenges and grief, she chose to *rest* in the Lord.

Though the mortal men she'd loved so dearly were gone, the immortal man she loved even more was closer than ever. Her eternal best friend, her anchor, her confidant, became the Lord Jesus. He was, after all, the one who'd already felt all her pain.

Today, decades after the year that nearly broke her, she feels a different kind of holy patience. Rather than waiting for the Lord to ease her burdens, she now waits patiently for a trio of reunions on the other side. And as the days pass, she finds comfort in the *rest*.

Invitation

Take time to count the significant blessings in your life and weigh them against the temporary trials. Study the scriptural and modern accounts of others who've endured similar, or even greater trials, and look for their patterns of patience. Schedule time to breathe, to ponder, and to find rest.

Other scriptures for consideration:

Behold, we count them happy which endure. Ye have heard of the patience of Job, and have seen the end of the Lord; that the Lord is very pitiful, and of tender mercy.
—James 5:11

He that is slow to wrath is of great understanding: but he that is hasty of spirit exalteth folly.
—Proverbs 14:29

PRAYERFULNESS

Ask, and it shall be given you;

SEEK,

and ye shall find; knock,

and it shall be opened unto you:

For every one that asketh receiveth;

and he that seeketh findeth;

and to him that knocketh it shall be opened.

—Matthew 7:7–8

More Holiness Give Me

Prayer is a pillar of the gospel of Jesus Christ. He taught us to pray in word and by example and so many years after His death and resurrection, it remains our most valuable conduit to heaven. No matter how crowded and noisy earthy communications become, the lifeline to His heavenly throne remains.

Jesus already knows us—perfectly, and in stunning detail we cannot imagine. And we come to know Him in our own humble, imperfect way through prayer. It's a simple truth.

For a moment, think about your greatest friends, the cherished few whose sentences you finish and whose trials you recognize. Those priceless relationships are based on the time you've spent together. If we desire the same closeness with Christ, we should spend time with Him. And one way we do that is in heartfelt prayer.

Still, the real beauty of this verse comes in the invitation to do more than simply pray and wait. We must *seek*, and when we do, there's a divine promise. Imagine the verse with another, less active verb. Look? Wander? Wonder? The use of *seek* pushes us from our comfort zones to exercise our spiritual muscles. Yes, we pray and ask. But then we do our part and actively *seek* solutions and answers.

A generation ago, a troubled wife learned the value of doing more than praying, but then partnering with God in *seeking* for answers. When her middle-aged, otherwise healthy and active husband became ill, answers from some of the finest doctors in America were few and far between. They prayed constantly, together and alone, for answers and healing. In time, his tired but persevering wife felt heaven whispering that she needed to more actively seek answers. She spent hours, day and night, thinking beyond what modern medicine offered.

She could have prayed and stayed on her knees. She could have visited others in need to lighten her load, done good around her, found rest in the Lord. In fact, she did all these things and still found strength to *seek* answers to their righteous pleadings. Her active, persistent asking and seeking led to a doctor more than a thousand miles from home. Over the course of a year, the answers they sought came on road trips and in unfamiliar doctors' offices and in miraculous, unconventional ways. Their prayers were answered, and he lives today, because they rejoiced not just in the prayers, but in the *seeking*.

Invitation

Study the questions on your mind and the prayers you've offered. Ask yourself whether you're simply waiting, or whether you're working. Yes, continue to spend time in prayer both day and night. But then look for opportunities to actively seek out answers. Embrace the energy of seeking out His will for you, and trust that He will always keep His promises and provide the answers you need when you need them.

Other scriptures for consideration:

But thou, when thou prayest, enter into thy closet, and when thou hast shut thy door, pray to thy Father which is in secret; and thy Father which seeth in secret shall reward thee openly.
—Matthew 6:6

God is our refuge and strength, a very present help in trouble.
—Psalm 46:1

FAITH

Now faith is the substance of things

HOPED

for, the evidence of things not seen.

—Hebrews 11:1

Finlandia (Be Still, My Soul)

Perhaps no attribute is more important in our quest to become better, bolder, more effective witnesses of Christ. Unless we witnessed it firsthand, as did the shepherds in the fields outside Bethlehem, we rely on faith to tell His story. Perhaps a few hundred had a personal experience and witnessed Christ in the flesh, either before or after His death and resurrection, but billions more either gone or living rely on faith for what they did not personally witness.

Read this verse and allow yourself to pause and punctuate the word hope. It's instructive that faith isn't a passive pursuit. We don't serve and stall, we don't pray and wait, we don't forgive and sleep. Like so many words in the good news of the gospel, faith inspires us to be agents of actions. *Hope* begs us to use faith not simply as a cure to swallow, but a workout regime for our spiritual health.

During the early months of the global pandemic, a husband and father found his faith on fumes. Crippled by closures and the endless news cycle, he didn't wake up with a faith crisis—instead, it seemed to slowly find him, like a persistent itch he couldn't reach.

He prayed, he read the scriptures, but he felt his tether to heaven had been cut. Then, one day, while once again on his knees and wondering if anyone was listening, this verse came to mind. He surveyed his faith. In his mind, he examined it from every angle. What had changed? Had he made choices that had dulled his once vibrant faith?

Done praying but still on his weary knees, the Spirit silently asked, *Do you still have hope? Do you still hope to know? Or have you decided to doubt?*

The sacred whispers moved him to tears and he asked aloud, "But how do I know? How do I know whether I still have *hope* or not?"

Once again the answer was simple and unmistakable: "Well, my son, you're on your knees all alone, aren't you?"

And just like that, the man's heart began to heal. His journey to fully restored faith took time, but the experience had reminded him of what he'd once known. As James teaches, faith without works is dead. Our friend in this sweet story might say the same thing about faith without *hope*.

Other scriptures for consideration:

Even so faith, if it hath not works, is dead, being alone. Yea, a man may say, Thou hast faith, and I have works: shew me thy faith without thy works, and I will shew thee my faith by my works.
—James 2:17–18

But Jesus turned him about, and when he saw her, he said, Daughter, be of good comfort; thy faith hath made thee whole. And the woman was made whole from that hour.
—Matthew 9:22

Invitation

As you learn to exercise and increase your faith, let hope be your guide. When your faith runs low, feel hope it will return. When the day doesn't unfold as planned, despite your great faith, hang on to hope that tomorrow will be better. Allow hope to rule and run your life. Never lose grip of your hope in Jesus Christ and in His plan.

As this written and musical adventure draws to a close, we leave you with what matters most.

Together we thank the One who makes all things possible. He is why we write, play, and perform. Jesus is the anchor of our art and the foundation of our families.

Though none of us were there on the day this all began, we know He lives.

We weren't there to hold Him, to bring gifts, or to watch Him grow.

But we know Jesus is real.

And even though we didn't see all the miracles then, we see them now, all around us.

We testify that Jesus Christ is the only begotten Son of God.

We testify that His ministry and gospel are as real now as they were in His ancient days.

We testify that He loves you deeply, personally, perfectly.

We believe with all our hearts that Jesus desires each of us to become even better friends with Him.

To know Him better.

To knock more often.

To seek more earnestly.

To walk more closely at His side.

Friends, in a world torn by divisions and despair, hunger and homelessness, may we each become modern-day witnesses of all we did not need to personally see in Bethlehem or Calvary.

May we testify of the greatest story ever told.

May we share the truth of the only spotless One and the only way back to our heavenly home.

May we live every single day of the rest of our lives as His disciples.

As witnesses of Christmas.

And, even more importantly, of Him.

He Lives!